ideals® COUNTRY

More Than 50 Years of Celebrating Life's Most Treasured Moments

Vol. 53, No. 4

"Warm, mellow summer—
The slowing sunbeams make every nerve tingle."

—John Muir

IDEALS—Vol. 53, No. 4 June MCMXCVI IDEALS (ISSN 0019-137X) is published eight times a year: February, March, May, June, August, September, November, December by IDEALS PUBLICATIONS INCORPORATED, 535 Metroplex Drive, Suite 250, Nashville, TN 37211. Second-class postage paid at Nashville, Tennessee, and additional mailing offices. Copyright © MCMXCVI by IDEALS PUBLICATIONS INCORPORATED. POSTMASTER: Send address changes to Ideals, PO Box 305300, Nashville, TN 37230. All rights reserved. Title IDEALS registered U.S. Patent Office.

SINGLE ISSUE—U.S. $5.95 USD; Higher in Canada
ONE-YEAR SUBSCRIPTION—8 issues—U.S. $19.95 USD; Canada $36.00 CDN (incl. GST and shipping); Foreign $25.95 USD
TWO-YEAR SUBSCRIPTION—16 issues—U.S. $35.95 USD; Canada $66.50 CDN (incl. GST and shipping); Foreign $47.95 USD

Printed and bound in USA by Quebecor Printing. Printed on Weyerhaeuser Husky.

The paper used in this publication meets the minimum requirements of
American National Standard for Information Sciences—Permanence of Paper for Printed Library Materials, ANSI Z39.48-1984.

Subscribers may call customer service at 1-800-558-4343 to make address changes.
Unsolicited manuscripts will not be returned without a self-addressed, stamped envelope.

ISBN 0-8249-1137-7   GST 131903775

Cover Photo: OLD OAKEN PUMP. Ken Dequaine, Photographer.

Inside Front Cover: GOLDEN GLORIES—GOLDFINCHES. Marc Hanson, artist.
Courtesy of the artist and Wild Wings, Inc., Lake City, Minnesota.

Inside Back Cover: DAY DREAMS. Lee Stroncek, artist.
Courtesy of the artist and Wild Wings, Inc., Lake City, Minnesota.

Early Morning

Isla Paschal Richardson

There's a spot in the woods that I wish you might see;
It slopes down the hillside—come stand there with me
Quite early some morning in June. The sun
Sprinkles diamonds on cobwebs the spiders have spun
Over wild morning-glories bespattered with dew.
I haven't the words to describe it to you.
Come join me some morn while the grass is still wet;
I'll show you a scene that you'll never forget.

Summer Sounds

Grace V. Watkins

A little wind came over the hill
With such a lovely, murmuring sound
That grasses, waiting green and still,
Bowed graciously; and a robin found
The notes of his tiny clarinet
In tune with the wind's soft minuet.

COSMOS, MORNING-GLORIES, AND ZINNIAS
Gastonia, North Carolina
Norman Poole Photography

The Misty Meadow

Margaret Ellen Jacob Rice

I walk the misty meadow
    In the glow of early dawn
And hear the birds awakening
    To sing their morning song.

A shim'ring rain of dewdrops
    Falls so gently to the ground,
And brightly blossomed flowers wave
    Their sleepy heads around.

The path that lies before me
    Wanders freely to and fro;
And gentle breezes pass me by
    With whispers as they go.

With wings of gold, the butterflies
    Dance freely in the air.
The dappled fawn looks startled
    And lifts his head to stare.

I sit down by the brooklet
    To daydream of life sublime;
How blessed to experience
    The meadow in her prime.

FOXGLOVE AND WILD MUSTARD
Del Norte County, California
Steve Terrill Photography

The Little Spring Flows Clear Again

Glenn Ward Dresbach

The little spring flows clear again
While I stand looking close to see
What clouded it. If wings were here
To splash the silver merrily,
They flew before I came too near.

And if a fawn had rubbed its nose,
Thrust deep in silver running cool,
Upon the bottom of the spring,
It heard me wading in the pool
Of shadow where the thrushes sing.

The little spring flows clear again
But now is clouded in my mind.
The flight of wings that went away,
And something that I came to find,
Was loveliness afraid to stay.

ROARING FORK STREAM
Great Smoky Mountains National Park, Tennessee
William Johnson
Johnson's Photography

Summer Small Talk

Lon Myruski

'Cross the summer meadows
Waft simple pleasantries,
Soft whispers 'tween the tall grass
And the passing breeze
Where crickets call to June bugs
And swaying willows sigh—
Beguiling summer small talk
To charm the passers-by.

Round a rippling millpond
Rise murmurings of frogs
Who've gathered there to gossip
On old mossy logs.
And dabbling ducks go quacking
Amidst these duckweed sprays—
Just idle summer small talk
To pass the time of day.

Chatty wrens and warblers
Commune in serenades,
Enchanting rustic rhythms
Eloquently phrased.
And to these summer places
I'm helplessly allured;
Enthralled by summer small talk,
I hang on every word.

GIRLS COLLECTING FLOWERS
Henry John Yeend King, 1855-1924
Bonhams, London
Superstock

Country CHRONICLE
—Lansing Christman—

YESTERYEAR'S MONTHS OF JUNE

June, with her blue sky and sun, lures me out into those bucolic country lanes far removed from the rush of cars on our busy thoroughfares. She puts my heart in tune with the rhythm of the universe. I sense the heartbeat of the land and hear the poetic muses of the rolling hills.

I have fond memories of many Junes; I have seen and lived so many of them. The young Junes were often spent picking wild strawberries with my mother in the old neglected fields where daisies and hawkweed and Queen Anne's lace were gracefully replacing the thinning timothy. The delightful aroma of the ripening berries filled the air around us.

In later Junes, vacations from school marked the beginning of summer days of work on the farm—cultivating acres of corn behind a horse-drawn cultivator, harvesting hay with a mowing machine pulled by a team, listening to the clicking of the racing knives in the cutting bar, seeing the hay fall in perfect swaths around a field, watching the hay rake leave those rhythmic, rounded windrows behind.

There were forty Junes spent at an office desk with clattering teletypes and ringing telephones; but I had my weekends and evenings in my home in the country. I had those evenings in the solace of the dusk when the wood thrush sang and the blinking lights of fireflies waltzed in the ballroom of the twilight hours.

Here now are my older Junes; yet they are the same ones I knew as a boy and as a man. June still charms me and lures me out into the outdoor world under blue, sunny skies. She soothes me with her songs, and I am young again.

The author of two published books, Lansing Christman has been contributing to Ideals *for more than twenty years. Mr. Christman has also been published in several American, foreign, and braille anthologies. He lives in rural South Carolina.*

ROLLED HAY
Cades Cove, Tennessee
Jeff Gnass Photography

TRAVELER'S
Diary

Laura K. Griffis

17 June, Saturday afternoon
Grand Teton National Park, Wyoming

What an exhilarating day! I spent the better part of the day floating happily on a raft down the Snake River, enjoying the majestic mountains and woodlands of Grand Teton National Park. I was hesitant at first to embark on any sort of "boat trip" in this wilderness, but our friendly tour guide reassured us city slickers that it was a gentle float trip, not a white-water expedition.

The weather was beautiful! Wyoming has a lovely climate in summer. I kept my camera ready all day, hoping to glimpse a sight of an elk or two left from the thousands that take refuge here each winter. Our tour guide told us all about the wonderful wildlife that fills this seemingly endless mountain valley. Bald eagles, trumpeter swans, and bison all make their homes here. I was lucky enough to spot a large blue heron wading through the water. Captivating!

After stopping on the shore for lunch (which we shared with some local chipmunks), I gazed at the distant, snow-capped peaks and listened to the cheerful songs of mountain bluebirds as they swooped from tree to tree. I soon forgot all about taking pictures, for I quickly lost myself in the wonders and serenity of this magical place.

LUPINE AND BALSAM ROOT
Grand Teton National Park, Wyoming
Norman Poole Photography

I Need a
Rendezvous
with Hills

Roy G. Rogers

I need a rendezvous with hills
    Where clouds walk in the sky.
I need to wrap myself in fog
    To look up and reach high.

I need communion in the woods,
    A sacrament to share
With birds and other wildwood things
    So free and happy there.

I need a breath of mountain air
    To sweep all cares away.
I need a rendezvous with hills
    And stars, where I can pray

And gain perspective on some peak,
    The forest as my shrine.
I need to hear God speak to me
    Beneath a singing pine.

The Seed

Myra P. Ellis

Once a seed that fell was lifted
By a passing breeze and drifted
    To this corner, by the rock.
Autumn sun and rain propelled it,
Mother Earth received and held it
    In a pocket of her frock.
Squatter's rights were undisputed;
And this summer, strongly rooted,
    Stands a sturdy hollyhock.

COLLECTOR'S CORNER

MAJOLICA

by Meghan Browning

When I was eight years old, my great grandmother decided to share her extensive collection of majolica with all her grandchildren. At my young age, I could barely pronounce the word *majolica*; yet I was mesmerized by the rich colors and delightful images that filled the china hutch where Grandmother kept her treasured pieces. Each grandchild was asked to choose just one piece from the shelves. I considered the array of teapots, plates, and pitchers carefully and graciously chose a small butter pat dish, no more than three inches in diameter. Its glazed surface displayed the face of a bright pansy, and it instantly brought a smile to my face. As a child, I happily used it to display loose wildflower petals; many years later it held butter at my first dinner party. I was always grateful to Grandmother for sharing her collection with me and for sparking my interest in the beauty and whimsy of majolica.

Throughout the years, I have added many more colorful majolica pieces to my own china hutch (always giving my pansy dish the most prominent spot). On the lower shelf is a navy blue pedestal dish adorned with geraniums and strawberries; next to it sits a humorous frog-shaped pitcher whose mouth pours my iced tea on hot summer days. I discovered my best find at an antique shop in New England. On a crowded shelf that was thick with glass bottles and tea cups, I spotted a circle of yellow buried in the back. I gingerly picked through the clutter to uncover the most charming majolica teapot I'd ever seen. It was covered with a shell and seaweed pattern. Once a part of a complete tea set, the pot bore the mark of a nineteenth-century American potter. I proudly placed the teapot next to my cherished butter pat dish and admired my majolica collection. Grandmother would be proud.

SUNFLOWER BOWL, Majolica, Griffen, Smith & Hill, ca. 1880-1890.
Chester County Historical Society, West Chester, Pennsylvania.
George J. Fistrovich, photographer.

GEORGE MORLEY'S MAJOLICA. EAST LIVERPOOL, O.

BENNETT'S JAN. 23, 1873. PATENT.

MORLEY & CO. MAJOLLICA WELLSVILLE, O.

EUREKA POTTERY TRENTON

DAISY COMPOTE, Majolica, Griffen, Smith & Hill, ca. 1880-1890.
Chester County Historical Society, West Chester, Pennsylvania.
George J. Fistrovich, photographer.

FACT CORNER

If you would like to start a majolica collection of your own, here are some facts you should know:

HISTORY

- Created by Herbert Minton, an English potter, in 1850 to resemble Renaissance pieces
- Named after *maiolica,* a sixteenth-century Italian lusterware
- Very popular among middle class during Victorian age
- Produced widely by British and American potteries between 1850 and 1890
- Last produced around 1912

DISTINGUISHING CHARACTERISTICS

- Ornate and often garish designs
- Organic designs often reflecting the piece's use:
  - a covered sardine serving dish topped with sculpted sardines and seaweed
  - a lettuce-leaf-shaped salad plate
  - an oyster plate covered with seashells
- Rich, deep-colored glazes
- Weight between lighter carnival ware and heavier stoneware
- Three raised marks often on underside of piece from three-legged stand used in kiln during firing
- Glaze sometimes crackled in appearance
- Potter's mark often on underside of piece (see examples on the opposite page)

FREQUENT PATTERNS

- Botanical designs—leaves, fruits, vegetables, wheat
- Animals—dogs, cats, birds, monkeys
- Garden themes—strawberries, flowers, latticework
- Whimsical figures—faces, angels, elves

INTERESTING PIECES

- Table serving pieces: game pie dishes, asparagus plates, cheese domes
- Home items: vases, calling card plates, spittoons, umbrella stands
- Garden decorations: seats, planters, cachepots

The Farm

Ruth H. Underhill

I'd love to go back to our farm
Where I scampered as a child.
I'd dash so swiftly through the fields
And pick daisies that grew wild.

Hiding twixt the rows of corn,
Climbing all the tallest trees,
I'd nap for hours high in the loft
Then skip sprightly 'cross the leas.

My cousins oft would visit me,
And I would show them all the fun.
We'd hunt for brown eggs ev'ry morn
And then have picnics in the sun.

Dashing to the rippling brook
Neath the swishing willow trees,
We'd soak up rays of golden sun
And dance with summer's soothing breeze.

Cruising in the cool creek bed
With our handsome homemade raft,
We'd sometimes spill out overboard—
Oh, we skittered and we laughed!

When dusk fell, we'd head back home,
Cutting through the fields of wheat.
We'd watch the sun set o'er the farm
And then sleep in a peace so sweet.

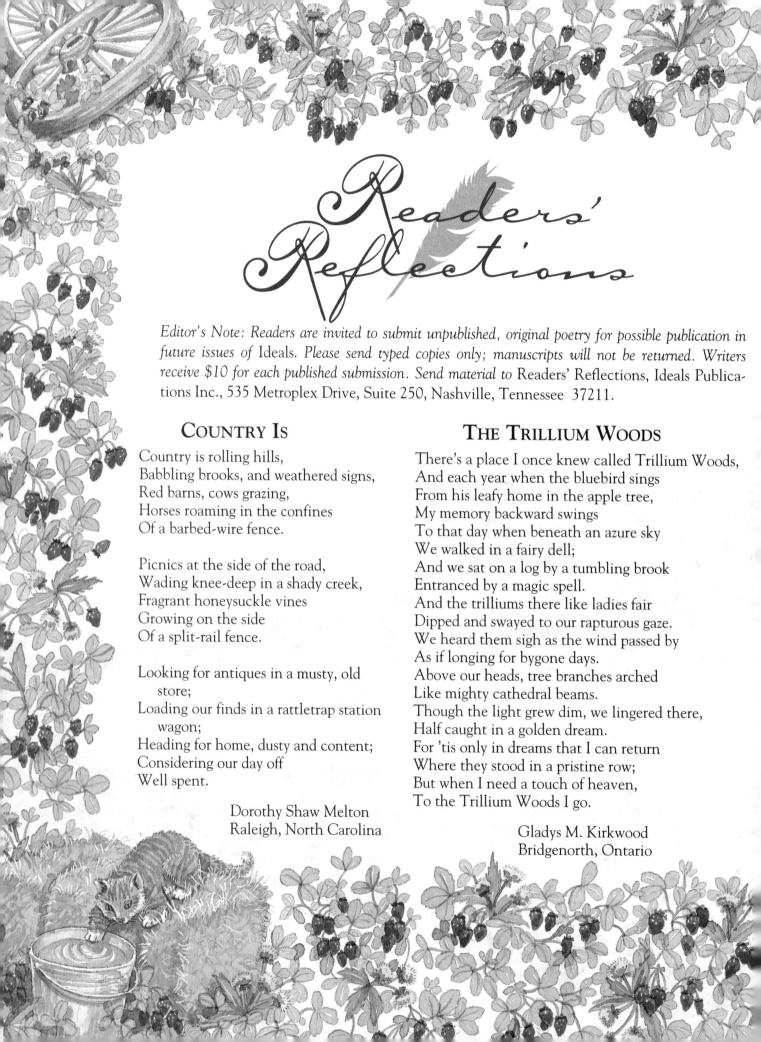

Readers' Reflections

Editor's Note: Readers are invited to submit unpublished, original poetry for possible publication in future issues of Ideals. Please send typed copies only; manuscripts will not be returned. Writers receive $10 for each published submission. Send material to Readers' Reflections, Ideals Publications Inc., 535 Metroplex Drive, Suite 250, Nashville, Tennessee 37211.

COUNTRY IS

Country is rolling hills,
Babbling brooks, and weathered signs,
Red barns, cows grazing,
Horses roaming in the confines
Of a barbed-wire fence.

Picnics at the side of the road,
Wading knee-deep in a shady creek,
Fragrant honeysuckle vines
Growing on the side
Of a split-rail fence.

Looking for antiques in a musty, old
　　store;
Loading our finds in a rattletrap station
　　wagon;
Heading for home, dusty and content;
Considering our day off
Well spent.

Dorothy Shaw Melton
Raleigh, North Carolina

THE TRILLIUM WOODS

There's a place I once knew called Trillium Woods,
And each year when the bluebird sings
From his leafy home in the apple tree,
My memory backward swings
To that day when beneath an azure sky
We walked in a fairy dell;
And we sat on a log by a tumbling brook
Entranced by a magic spell.
And the trilliums there like ladies fair
Dipped and swayed to our rapturous gaze.
We heard them sigh as the wind passed by
As if longing for bygone days.
Above our heads, tree branches arched
Like mighty cathedral beams.
Though the light grew dim, we lingered there,
Half caught in a golden dream.
For 'tis only in dreams that I can return
Where they stood in a pristine row;
But when I need a touch of heaven,
To the Trillium Woods I go.

Gladys M. Kirkwood
Bridgenorth, Ontario

BUSH ROAD

Along the bush road's leafy lanes,
Majestic maples soar in space,
Huge hemlocks line the winding way,
And white barked birches glow with grace.

The sighing cedars bar the breeze
That makes the pallid poplars quiver,

And bushy balsams crowd the creek
That winds its way down to the river.

Beneath the boughs, there's a silence still
And peace that sets a soul at ease.
God's presence can be plainly felt
Beneath high towering, ageless trees.

E. A. Godfrey
Victoria, British Columbia

WALKING WITH GRANDPA

My grandpa can't be beat,
Specially down a country lane
With clover round our feet.
When we go walking down a lane
He always seems to know
Just where the vi'lets are hiding
And where the peonies grow.
He's the first to see a butterfly
Or hear a meadowlark;
And he can tell which way is north
By the trees with their green bark.
He knows which trees the owls sleep in
And the ones where bees store honey;
And he shows me holes in the ground
Where the rabbits raise their bunnies.
He tells me to remember
That everything we see
Is a gift from a loving God
To folks like him and me.
The best part of the walking
Is holding Grandpa's hand
And looking up as he looks down.
And we both wink and understand
That we are special to each other
And know we'll always be,
For we love one another
With a love that's plain to see.

John J. Pepping
Los Angeles, California

SUMMER CHILD

A week ago fair June was born,
And now my glad heart sings.
With beauty of a newborn child
She lifts the earth on wings,
Comes tripping in with rosy lips,
A daisy in her hair
And in her hand a butterfly,
A face so very fair.
With lady's-slippers on her feet
And bluebells in her eyes,
She skips along through meadows dull
And gazes at the skies.
Each place breathes; each place she steps
Is left a living green.
She brushes pussy willows' coats
And leaves a silver sheen.
She trips across the meadow green
And touches earth to hand,
And everywhere she chances to touch
Leaves flowers on the land.
Her soothing breath will warm the earth;
She bids the winter flee.
She walks the skyway with the sun
And makes the summer be.

Joy Cassano
Federalsburg, Maryland

Across the Meadow

Olive Dunkelberger

From far across the meadow
Stands a barn of simple grace
Wherein a farmer's treasures
Are counted and kept in place.

His livelihood depends upon
A working plan with God
When sun and shower alternate
To feed the hungry sod.

I see a fence of wooden rails,
A landmark of the past;
The architect had vision then
In knowing it would last.

I see a crib for storing corn;
I see a shop for tools;
And there's the shed for wagons
That were hitched to sturdy mules.

The rambling house has firmly stood
Through five score years or more
With dignity and simple charm
Since the carefree days of yore.

I still recall my childhood there
When memory turns the years,
And the joys of youth come calling
Mid a shower of gentle tears.

If I could walk with yesteryear across the meadow fair
Back to the farm of memory and the joys that linger there,
I would live again in harmony with the elements of time
And feel a spiritual comfort in this aging heart of mine.

PERENNIAL BORDER GARDEN
Merrimack County, New Hampshire
William Johnson
Johnson's Photography

YOUNG GARDENER. Superstock.

A Garden So Rich

Christie Craig

I watched out the window as they started turning over the soil. Of course, my husband did most of the work while our five-year-old son spent most of his energy fingering through the dirt looking for worms. Still, the sight of the two of them "working" side by side, preparing the ground for a summer garden, brought a smile to my face.

For just a moment I considered joining them.

Then I remembered the excitement I'd heard in my son's voice when he announced, "Saturday morning me and Daddy are going to plant a garden!"

I sipped my coffee wondering if joining in on the fun would be interfering. Right then I heard my son call out, "Hey, Dad, bet you can't find a worm this fine."

"Oh yeah? Look at this one," my husband countered with a grin.

I could see the two squirming creatures that dangled from their fingers in some sort of "fine" worm contest. For a second I wondered how one went about qualifying a fine worm. Cringing, I made up my mind. This was their project, I'd leave it to them. Besides, it might be more fun to stand back and simply see what grows out of this garden.

I watched as they poked the seeds into the black topsoil. Carefully, they planted tomatoes, squash, and green beans. I listened to the spurts of laughter, the dialogue that passed back and forth.

"When will they grow, Daddy?"

"Soon," my husband replied.

"Tonight?"

"Not that soon."

"Tomorrow?" my son asked.

"In a few days. The seeds have to sprout, then grow."

"Then we'll have vegetables?"

"No, it takes a while."

"One day?" my son questioned.

"Longer," my husband replied.

"Two days?" his anxious, young voice queried.

I saw the smile touch my husband's expression, and at that moment I knew I was already seeing the first of many fruits the garden would bring. My son would learn that some things in life weren't instant. My husband would learn how to better deal with a five-year-old's expectations and endless questions. Patience—what a wonderful fruit to grow.

Throughout the next week, they often knelt to the ground and looked for signs of new life. The sight of them, so close and with common goals, warmed my heart and made me happy I'd decided to watch from afar.

More days passed, and each afternoon I watched the two of them water their garden. My son always managed to get as wet as the garden; and, more times than not, even my husband came in drenched. The laughter that followed them made the muddy tracks and the extra laundry tolerable.

Finally, the plants appeared. From the distance I enjoyed my son's look of glee, as well as the look of wonder on my husband's face as he, too, watched our son. And like the tiny plants breaking through the earth, I saw fruit number two appear. Pride—what a wonderful fruit to grow.

The weeks passed; the garden grew. At the first fruit-bearing blossoms, I watched the two men in my life study and examine each plant. My son would ask questions, and my husband would do his best to explain.

"Why do they call squash, 'squash?' " the smaller and dirtier gardener questioned.

"I don't know," came my husband's answer.

"I wonder how many worms live in this garden?" my son asked.

"I don't know," my husband replied.

"A million?"

"Probably," my husband said.

"Can we catch them?" Excitement radiated from his voice.

"I don't think so," the older gardener answered with a chuckle. "But look at this blossom."

"Will it really become a tomato?" came yet another question.

"It will," my husband smiled.

I smiled too. For I knew I was watching not only a garden but also a relationship take root—watching cherished moments being framed for future memories.

They continued to water, to weed, and to care for their small garden. And after all the work and effort, they proudly produced ten tomatoes, two medium squash, and three pots of beans.

One afternoon, my husband stared out the window at the wilting plants and asked, "Was it all worth it?"

Our smiles met at the same time. There was no need to answer. Relationships, memories, patience, and pride. Who knew a garden could bear so much?

A SLICE OF LIFE

Edgar A. Guest

FISHERMAN

'Tis good to go a-fishing on river, lake or sea,
The flying gulls above you, and the waves just as free,
Away from wheels of commerce and smoke of factory stack,
A day of joy before you and duty at your back.

'Tis good to go a-fishing, when skies above are blue,
Out of the long year's sheaf of days to pilfer one or two;
To have no thought of money, no urge for worldly fame,
To be at heart a fisherman, and a fisherman by name.

Men see you from the distance, and this is all they say:
"There goes another fisherman. May luck be his today!"
And be you rich or be you poor they have no wish to know,
For all the world is friendly to the men who fishing go.

So let me be a fisherman. No other rank I'll seek,
The care-free man upon the bay of whom the travelers speak;
For there is envy in their eyes which kings may never know,
And every stranger cries, "Good luck!" to men who fishing go.

Edgar A. Guest began his illustrious career in 1895 at the age of fourteen when his work first appeared in the Detroit Free Press. His column was syndicated in over 300 newspapers, and he became known as "The Poet of the People."

Country Boy

Pearl D. Anderson

Little man of the soil
Yet to know of work and toil,
Laughing in the summer rain,
Playing with the golden grain,

Wondering at the seeds that grow,
Fruit and flowers for to show.
Work and pride await you here—
God and love and none to fear.

Lend to me for one small while
Sunshine of your freckled smile.
Through your laughing eyes so clear,
Show me my own yesteryear.

"God Almighty first planted a garden; and indeed, it is the purest of human pleasures."

—Francis Bacon

"One is nearer God's heart in a garden than anywhere else on earth."

—Dorothy Frances Gurney

Garden Partner

Margaret Rorke

I own a garden.
I plant and I hoe,
But I've a partner
I think you might know.

He mixes seasons
And ripens my seeds.
For His own reasons
He adds a few weeds.

He gives me sunshine
And showers and soil,
Sparks my ambition
And ardor to toil,

Nods at my pride in
The things I have grown,
And smiles when I speak
Of the garden "I" own.

Especially Father

Gladys Taber

In California, Father set up his little family in a tent in Tent City. We went swimming every day. I floated in the salt greenish water, keeping up by clinging with one hand to his shoulder. I was too young to swim, but I could go anywhere with Father doing the breast stroke powerfully beside me.

We bought oranges in washtubs at twenty-five cents a tub. This impressed me because Father and Mother kept marveling at it. The New England Christmas orange was a long way from this. Cooking was sketchy. We bought food at a delicatessen, and I thought store potato salad in a cardboard box was simply wonderful.

But the best was walking the beach with Father. Every shell was a mystery and a story. The seaweed was a book in itself, as Father talked about it. I gathered the long cool rubbery strands, filled my pockets with sand dollars and small pale shells, and struggled after Father's rapid steps. It's possible that he was out of a job, for we must have been poorer than usual, but my world was furnished richly with the gifts of the sea.

Even the grains of sand were wonderful, for Father could sift out the shining grains and talk about the time they were rocks and what happened to them in the long sweep of centuries.

The stars overhead had their romance, too. Everything visible to man's eye was a marvel. The great tides moved by the moon excited Father, so did the track of a small greenish snail on wet sand.

Rhyme
FOR FATHER'S DAY
Charles L. H. Wagner

Man's custom is to honor
The mothers of the race,
But fathers often warrant
Some condescending grace.
They seldom seek the limelight
For services they give
And ask no recognition
For the useful lives they live.

Their happiness is mostly
Achieved in children's love,
And selflessness they pattern
By Him who rules above.
To them the highest guerdons
Are family peace and joy;
And though the world forgets them,
Their best they still employ.

So let us honor fathers
And grant to them one day
When we can voice affection
In some small, special way.
Though they themselves may never
Exact what is their due,
Their hearts well up with gladness
When love's expressed and true.

GRANDDAD AND I

Georgia B. Adams

Down on the farm where Granddad lived
I spent many a day.
As if it were but yesterday,
I still can hear him say,
"Come, lad, let's go a-fishing"; and
As quick as one, two, three,
I'd fall in step beside him with
My heart tiptop with glee!

He knew the forests all by heart;
And so the day would come
When we would go a-nutting, and
We'd share a heap of fun!
Yes, Granddad was a busy man,
But somehow in some way
He shared my childhood moments, Ah!
It seems but yesterday!

THE ROCKER

Kathleen Y. Bergeron

My grandpa had a rocking chair
He sat in all the time.
He always shared it willingly
When in his lap I'd climb.

He'd tell me tales about his past;
I'd talk about my day
As happily together
In the chair we'd gently sway.

I liked to perch upon his knee,
My head against his arm;
I always knew while I was there,
I'd never come to harm.

My grandpa's gone for many years;
But I can clearly see
That rocker and my grandpa,
And both are holding me.

Before Reveille

Jean Rasey

His thoughts are of the farm, the quiet blend
Of evening lanes. The stream, where willows bend,
Runs down its slim bed like a vesper chime,
Meandering under boughs at starlight time,
Across the farmland, peace in its low song.
A brown owl stirs the leaves where, erelong
Tonight, a soft wind may be billowing through
Spice-laden orchards, rich with apple dew.

He thinks of beauty greater than the charm
His boyhood knew upon the valley farm:
The zigzag trail, the fruited underbrush,
The unexpectedness, the sudden hush
Of breathing when a wild deer comes to drink,
To nibble brook-mints at the water's brink.

For dearer than the heartbeat in his throat
Or badge of valor on this lad's rough coat
Is hope of lasting peace, the knowledge when
The smell of loam may stir for him again,
With song of brooks to sound the taps of day,
Of larks the reveille of dawn-lit gray.

FIELDS OF CORN
Haverhill, New Hampshire
William Johnson
Johnson's Photography

BITS & PIECES

A thoughtful mind . . . sees not the flag only,
but the nation itself . . . the principles,
the truths, the history.
— *Henry Ward Beecher*

*N*o nation is better than the
individuals that compose it.
— *Cordell Hull*

*W*here the Spirit of the Lord is, there is liberty.
— *II Corinthians 3:17*

*P*ersonal liberty is the paramount essential to
human dignity and human happiness.
— *Edward George Earle Bulwer-Lytton*

I believe in democracy because it releases
the energies of every human being.
— *Woodrow Wilson*

*W*ith malice toward none;
    with charity for all . . . let us strive
    on to finish the work we are in . . .
    to do all which may achieve
    and cherish a just and lasting peace
    among ourselves and with all nations.
        —*Abraham Lincoln*

*I*nscription on the Statue of Liberty:
    Give me your tired, your poor,
    Your huddled masses, yearning to breathe free,
    The wretched refuse of your teeming shore.
    Send these, the homeless, tempest-tossed to me,
    I lift my lamp beside the golden door!
        —*Emma Lazarus*

*P*roclaim liberty throughout all the land
    unto all the inhabitants thereof.
        —*Leviticus 25:10*

I am not a Virginian but an American.
        —*Patrick Henry*

MY NATIVE LAND

Walter E. Isenhour

America, my native land,
   I love thee more and more.
I love thy scenery so grand
   And view it o'er and o'er;
For there is majesty sublime
   From mountaintop to sea—
A land whose beauty and whose clime
   Is good enough for me.

America, I praise thee now,
   My native land so dear;
Unto thy noble flag I bow
   And lift my voice to cheer.
And may the God who gave us birth
   Protect and keep us free
From all dictatorship of earth
   Where men delight to be.

Let poets sing thy worthy praise
   And artists paint thy sky,
And may thy sons and daughters raise
   A standard that is high

In honor, honesty, and right
   To match thy every scene;
And let them labor with their might
   To keep thee pure and clean.

I love the beauty of thy hills,
   Thy mountains high and grand,
With all thy crystal, sparkling rills
   That flow across the land,
With flowers that grow along their brink,
   And trees so great and tall
That make thy nature-lovers think
   Of God who made them all.

I love thy patriotic sons
   Who fought for freedom's cause,
Who fell by cannon, sword, or guns
   To save thy sacred laws.
For by their sacrifice of life
   They saved from awful fate,
And gave to us from out the strife
   A nation grand and great.

FLAG SONG

Lydia Avery Coonley Ward

Out on the breeze,
O'er land and seas,
A beautiful banner is streaming,
Shining its stars,
Splendid its bars,
Under the sunshine 'tis gleaming.
Hail to the flag,
The dear, bonny flag—
The flag that is red, white, and blue.

Over the brave
Long may it wave,
Peace to the world ever bringing,
While to the stars
Linked with the bars
Hearts will forever be singing:
Hail to the flag,
The dear, bonny flag—
The flag that is red, white, and blue.

The unique perspective of Russ Flint's artistic style has made him a favorite of Ideals *readers for many years. A resident of California and father of four, Russ Flint has illustrated a children's Bible and many other books.*

AMERICA
Myrtie Fisher Seaverns

America! America!
   Land ever dear to me,
Land where the Pilgrims sought retreat
   And planted liberty.

O beautiful America!
   Your wonders never cease,
The beauties of both land and sea
   And sweet content and peace.

The beauty of the low foothills
   Beyond the fertile plain
And lofty mountains looking down
   On fields of golden grain.

The mighty rivers rushing on
   To join the ocean wide,
The many placid lakes and streams
   That dot the countryside.

The grandeur of the forest dense
   Where not a sound is heard
Except soft whispers of the trees
   Or singing of a bird.

The majesty of ocean might,
   Whose billows surge and roar
And then in baffled fury dash
   Against the rocky shore.

The tranquil peace of little towns
   Nestled on every side,
The white church perched upon the hill
   Where God seems to abide.

The Pilgrims planted freedom's seed
Then nurtured its faint gleam;
Its benefits we now enjoy,
Fulfillment of their dream.

My beautiful America!
The great hope of the West;
How oft you've been the promised land
To the hopeless and oppressed.

May your conscience ever guide you
And hold you staunch and true;
May you keep Old Glory flying high—
The Red and White and Blue.

America! America!
God guided you all the way;
The greatest country on the earth—
Our grand, old U.S.A.

LEGENDARY AMERICANS

NANCY SKARMEAS

SUSAN B. ANTHONY

As she approached the end of her life, Susan B. Anthony could look around her and see thousands of young, educated women filling seats at women's rights conventions and cheering speeches calling on the American government to recognize women's right to vote. Many of these young women had been inspired to support women's suffrage by Anthony herself, and their education and self-awareness represented a giant leap forward in the cause of rights for women in America. Yet Anthony more often than not found herself dissatisfied with these earnest young women. To them—many of whom had husbands and families and comfortable homes—women's suffrage was a cause to which they happily lent a few

hours here and there. To Anthony—who never married or had children and who labored for more than fifty years in the name of women's suffrage—achieving the vote for women was not merely a cause but the all-consuming focus for her life.

Susan Brownell Anthony was born on her family's farm near Adams, in western Massachusetts, in 1820. The activism and passion for women's equality that would characterize her adult life had their roots in the early lessons she learned from her parents. Daniel and Lucy Read Anthony were both ardent abolitionists; from their work to end slavery in America, Susan learned about courage, conviction, and respect for all humanity. Daniel Anthony, a Quaker, instilled in his daughter the Quaker belief that men and women were equal in the eyes of God; and in the Quaker women who spoke openly and forcefully in their community, Susan had role models unavailable to most girls of her era. She also had the example of her mother, a passionate, principled woman who attended the first women's rights convention at Seneca Falls, New York.

The Anthonys encouraged their daughter to be inquisitive and independent. As a child, Susan Anthony worked alongside the young women in her father's cotton mill and began to identify with working women. As a young adult, she taught school to earn extra income for the family and managed her father's farm; both experiences taught her the value of work, independence, and self-sufficiency while at the same time opening her eyes to the inequality women faced in the workplace. By the time she reached adulthood, Susan Anthony was a woman with a true passion for social issues. Her extraordinary childhood had prepared her to leave her mark upon the world.

In 1852, at age thirty-two, Anthony discovered a focus for her zeal and a purpose for her life. Two years earlier, she had met women's rights activist Elizabeth Cady Stanton, who had urged Anthony to channel her intelligence, education, and energy into the cause of women's suffrage. Anthony resisted; she believed that her energies were more practically directed toward the temperance movement, a cause to which she had devoted several years. Anthony became a confirmed suffragist when, despite her status as a leading member of the Daughters of Temperance, she was refused, due to her gender, the right to speak at a temperance rally in New York. Denied a voice, Anthony came to understand a basic truth about the place of women in American society: until American women achieved equal representation under the law, they could have little influence on American life. From that day forward, Anthony, in partnership with Stanton, devoted her life to achieving the vote for American women.

The two women became an inspirational team. Stanton was an eloquent orator and a brilliant writer, a master of rhetoric who inspired all whom she met. Anthony became her organizer and her tactician. Although she never developed into a powerful speaker and was not blessed with a charismatic personality, Susan Anthony's tireless work became the backbone of the women's suffrage movement.

In 1868, Anthony and Stanton began the newspaper *Revolution,* which was devoted to promoting suffrage and other women's issues. Anthony and Stanton called for equal pay for equal work, better education for young girls, and equal employment opportunities for women.

In 1869, Anthony and Stanton formed the National Women's Suffrage Association, and Anthony began thirty years of travel across the United States in support of a constitutional amendment recognizing women's right to vote. Progress on the amendment was slow and painstaking; and Anthony suffered much criticism and abuse from men and women alike who, due to her unmarried state and rather dour appearance, called her a bitter old maid with nothing better to do than stir up trouble. Yet her commitment never wavered. Anthony lived these years with no true place to call home, with no family of her own, and with no concessions to personal needs or private life; she had taken to heart her belief that until women gained a voice in American society, there could be no other focus for their energies and efforts.

Susan B. Anthony attended her last women's rights convention in February of 1906 at the age of eighty-six. She died the following month. In many ways, she had seen little progress for all the hard work of her life. By 1906, only four states had acknowledged the right of their female citizens to vote; and the Nineteenth Amendment, which recognized the right of all American women to vote, was still fourteen years away. Although she must have felt a great measure of discouragement and frustration, Anthony never lost hope. She left the women at her final convention with the rallying cry, "Failure is impossible."

Nearly a century after Susan B. Anthony's death and three quarters of a century after the passage of the Nineteenth Amendment, American women still talk about the issues that were foremost on her mind—equal pay for equal work, equal employment opportunities for women, and better education for girls. The difference is that today every American woman can address these issues through the power of the vote. Without the courage, passion, and sacrifice of Susan B. Anthony, this most basic of rights surely would have eluded American women for many more years.

Susan B. Anthony understood that issues of social equality for women could not be honestly addressed as long as the only voices recognized by the government were those of its male citizens. She truly gave her life to guaranteeing women the most basic right in any democracy, the right to vote. Today, American women can best honor her legacy by the small but powerful act of casting a ballot.

Nancy Skarmeas is a book editor and mother of a newborn son, Gordon, who is keeping her and her husband quite busy at their home in New Hampshire. Her Greek and Irish ancestry has fostered a lifelong interest in research and history.

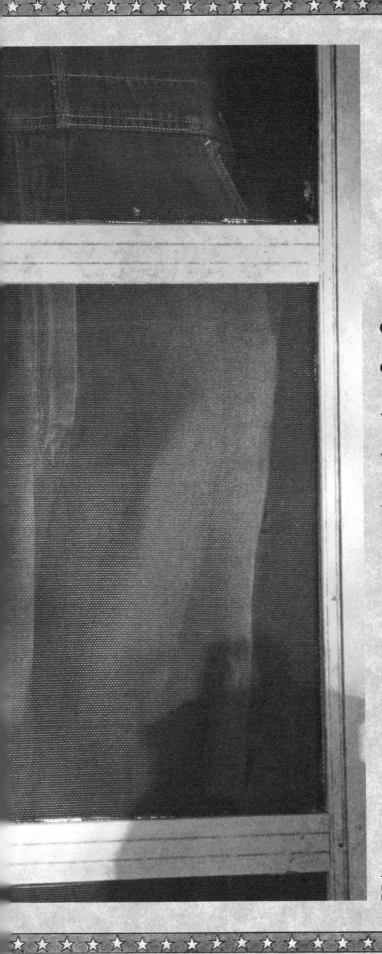

A Slice of
Buttered Bread

Inez Culver Corbin

Our way of living is the best.
    We like the special brand
Of freedom that we now enjoy
    In our united land.

We have the chance to voice our thoughts,
    To heed a church bell's call,
To hear spring laughter through the rain
    And watch the crops grow tall.

With warm sun on the roof, the peace
    Of starlight overhead,
A pillowed chair, a lighted lamp,
    A slice of buttered bread.

Our way of living is the best,
    Which we would always choose.
But we must strive for it with faith
    And courage, lest we lose

The dear associations of
    Our home, the right to keep
A safe place where a little child
    May sing himself to sleep.

Ideals' Family Recipes

Favorite Recipes from the Ideals Family of Readers

Editor's Note: Please send us your best-loved recipes! Mail a typed copy of the recipe along with your name, address, and phone number to Ideals magazine, ATTN: Recipes, P.O. Box 305300, Nashville, Tennessee 37230. We will pay $10 for each recipe used. Recipes cannot be returned.

CAKE ICE-CREAM CONES

Preheat oven to 350° F. In a large bowl, prepare the batter of one 18¼-ounce box yellow cake mix according to the package directions, adding egg and oil as instructed; set aside. Place 20 flat-bottom ice-cream cones on an ungreased cookie sheet. Fill ⅔ of each cone with batter. Bake 20-25 minutes or until toothpick inserted in center of cone comes out clean. When cool, spread with white frosting and decorate with candy sprinkles.

Mrs. Ann Gergel
Olean, New York

GRAHAM CRACKER ICE CREAM

In a large bowl, combine 2 cups graham cracker crumbs, 2 cups whipping cream, 2 cups half and half, 1 cup sugar, 2 teaspoons vanilla, and 2¾ teaspoons almond extract; mix well. Freeze until solid but not hard. Beat mixture with an electric mixer until fluffy. Pour into 2 metal ice cube trays with the inserts removed or into an 8-inch-square, metal pan. Freeze 2 hours. Makes 9 servings.

Isabella Gibbs
North Wilkesboro, North Carolina

CLASSIC BANANA SPLIT

In an individual dessert dish, place 2 banana halves. Top banana with 1 scoop each of strawberry, chocolate, and vanilla ice cream. Drizzle 2 tablespoons caramel topping and 2 tablespoons chocolate syrup over ice cream. Sprinkle with 1 tablespoon chopped, toasted almonds. Top with whipped cream and 1 maraschino cherry. Makes 1 serving.

Joyce Tynes
Pascagoula, Mississippi

NUTTY ICE-CREAM SUNDAE DESSERT

Preheat oven to 350° F. In an 8-inch, square baking dish, melt ⅓ cup butter or margarine. Add ¾ cup butter-flavored cracker crumbs and mix well. Press crumb mixture firmly against bottom of dish. Bake 8 to 10 minutes or until bubbly. Cool slightly.

In a large mixing bowl, combine one 4-serving size package instant butter pecan pudding mix and ¾ cup milk. Beat on high speed for 2 minutes or until mixture thickens. Add 2 pints softened vanilla ice cream. Pour mixture over prepared crust. Crush 1 cup chocolate-covered peanuts and sprinkle over dessert. Freeze 3 hours or until firm. Makes 9 servings.

Margaret Anderson
Dunkerton, Iowa

OATMEAL COOKIE ICE CREAM PIE

Preheat oven to 350° F. Spray a 9-inch pie pan with vegetable cooking spray; set aside. In a large bowl, combine 1 cup chopped walnuts, 1 cup quick-cooking rolled oats, ¾ cup all-purpose flour, and ½ cup firmly packed brown sugar; mix well. Stir in ½ cup melted butter; mix well. Press mixture into prepared pan, building up rim. Bake 10 minutes; cool. Spread 1 cup seedless raspberry jam over bottom of crust. Spoon ½ gallon softened vanilla ice cream over jam. Freeze until firm. Let stand at room temperature 10 minutes before slicing. Makes 8 servings.

Nancy Bacon
Poland, Ohio

Remember When

BLUE MOON ICE CREAM
Lisa C. Ragan

On sticky summer evenings when my parents were feeling especially spontaneous, they'd load me and my brother, Mike, into the station wagon and head to Bert T. Owen's Ice Cream Parlor. It took me years to understand the name of the place, since Dad always said, "Let's go down to Bert-T's." As soon as we got there, I'd race in and carefully consider each and every flavor before choosing, every time, blue moon. I don't know what flavor that was, exactly; it was just something cool and sweet, and I thought it was the most beautiful shade of blue. It wasn't a very strong blue, not like robin's egg blue, but rather it had the suggestion of blue, almost like it glowed. I imagined that I was eating a piece of the moon.

Dad usually ordered something interesting, like rocky road. Mom was a faithful chocolate fan, and Mike always chose strawberry. He may as well have been getting vanilla in my opinion; so boring was his predictable selection. At twelve, he was six years

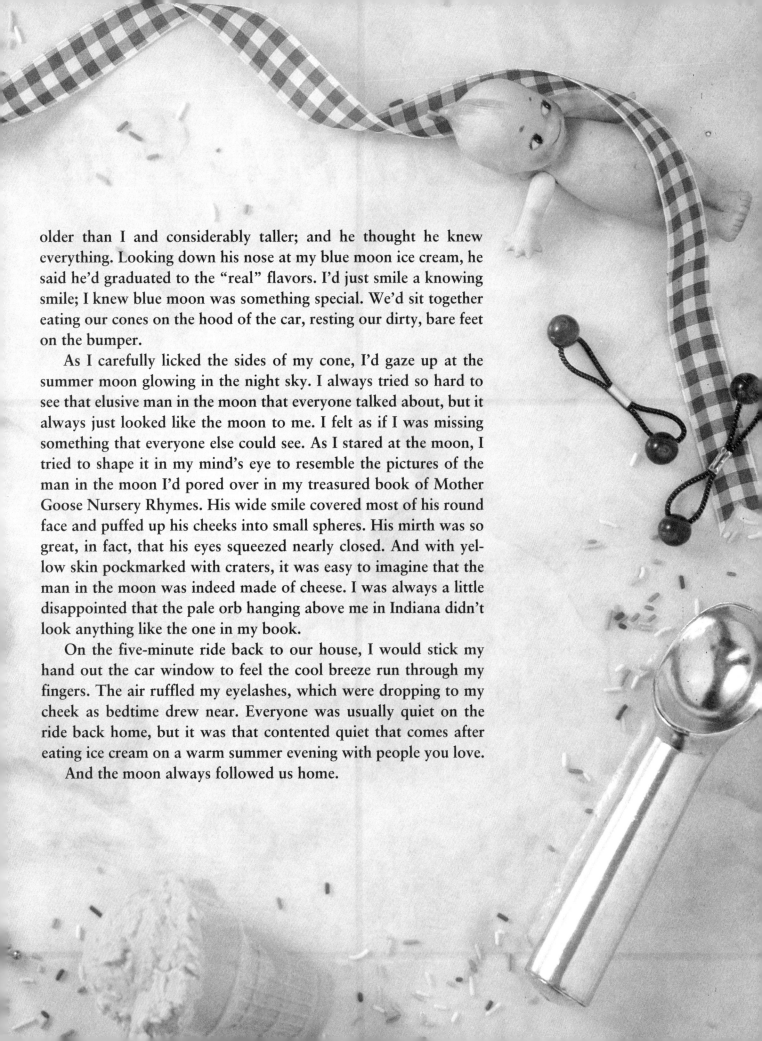

older than I and considerably taller; and he thought he knew everything. Looking down his nose at my blue moon ice cream, he said he'd graduated to the "real" flavors. I'd just smile a knowing smile; I knew blue moon was something special. We'd sit together eating our cones on the hood of the car, resting our dirty, bare feet on the bumper.

As I carefully licked the sides of my cone, I'd gaze up at the summer moon glowing in the night sky. I always tried so hard to see that elusive man in the moon that everyone talked about, but it always just looked like the moon to me. I felt as if I was missing something that everyone else could see. As I stared at the moon, I tried to shape it in my mind's eye to resemble the pictures of the man in the moon I'd pored over in my treasured book of Mother Goose Nursery Rhymes. His wide smile covered most of his round face and puffed up his cheeks into small spheres. His mirth was so great, in fact, that his eyes squeezed nearly closed. And with yellow skin pockmarked with craters, it was easy to imagine that the man in the moon was indeed made of cheese. I was always a little disappointed that the pale orb hanging above me in Indiana didn't look anything like the one in my book.

On the five-minute ride back to our house, I would stick my hand out the car window to feel the cool breeze run through my fingers. The air ruffled my eyelashes, which were dropping to my cheek as bedtime drew near. Everyone was usually quiet on the ride back home, but it was that contented quiet that comes after eating ice cream on a warm summer evening with people you love.

And the moon always followed us home.

The County Fair

Laurie Dawson

We worked all year for this event
　　And put aside our best—
Sweet jellies, pickles, household goods,
　　And linens in the chest.

The rivalry was often keen
　　Among the ones who canned;
The rosy fruit was placed just so
　　And labeled then by hand.

Our neighbor took her relish fine,
　　The green, the ripe, the hot;
And every year a ribbon blue
　　Each tempting jar begot.

Mom's best dill pickles stayed so plump,
  Their taste could not be beat;
She was sure to bring home prizes
  From our own county seat.

The fancy quilts were wrapped with care,
  Each one a brilliant beauty.
I'd hate to have the judge's job;
  It was a solemn duty!

Horse racing, husking, and calling hogs,
  Pitching horseshoes to and fro,
Or watching athletes climb a pole
  Was more fun than the show.

Prize-winning dresses were so sharp;
  The cakes were iced with flair.
And even when I won no prize,
  I loved the county fair!

THROUGH MY WINDOW

Pamela Kennedy
Art by Russ Flint

THE JOYS OF VACATION BIBLE SCHOOL

Every year when June rolls around and the evenings stretch longer, I begin to gird my loins for an inevitable summer ritual—vacation Bible school. In my religious traditions, vacation Bible school is as predictable as the summer hurricane season and only a little less daunting!

In April the supply list comes out for vacation Bible school, popularly referred to as VBS; and I begin saving things I would otherwise designate as trash: egg cartons, empty toilet paper rolls, juice can lids, fabric scraps, margarine tubs, and milk cartons. Some gifted craftsperson has ways of turning all this stuff into inspirational artifacts to be carted off to someone else's home and displayed on the kitchen wall or countertop. I guess vacation Bible school is the church's answer to recycling!

By May the literature arrives; and those of us willing to serve as teachers receive packets of brightly colored lesson plans, posters, and instructional materials designed by someone in Minneapolis, Minnesota, who has a Ph.D. in theology or religious education. Most VBS workers, however, do not have a Ph.D. in anything and are mostly concerned with getting through the week with their sanity intact and all those little pieces of shell macaroni glued on the right places in the Sea of Galilee scene.

After a few weeks of wading through the materials, the VBS director, usually a woman of saintly character and undying optimism, gathers all her teachers and workers. She delivers an inspiring talk about leaving a lasting impression on the little ones sent our way in the coming week, then she gives out the class lists. We teachers are then free to go to our rooms to decorate and set up. This is both my most feared and favorite part of VBS. I fear it because I am not a very artistic person. My decor tends toward the minimalist genre. I usually tack up the posters from the teacher's kit and loop a little crepe paper around the room. Then I sit in the childless quiet and contemplate all the wonderful spiritual lessons I will impart—that's my favorite part. I imagine eager little faces upturned to the sunshine of God's love, little minds unfolding like flowers as we read the Scriptures together. I write the names on my attendance chart, wondering what Bethany will be like, or Jason, or Crystal. Sixteen little people will invade my life and occupy my mornings for the next week, and at this point I love them all.

The first day of vacation Bible school is always chaos. Children who have never been in a church mingle with those who know the place inside and out. A few get upset because they aren't in the same class as their best friends. Someone usually falls down or throws up. The teachers aren't sure who goes to the craft tables when, and none of the sound equipment functions properly. Aside from these things, all else goes pretty much according to plan.

As the week progresses, I learn much about my little charges. I learn that Michael and Ben cannot be seated within ten feet of one another. I learn that I must have exactly the same number and kinds of stickers for each child, not eight of one and eight of another. I learn that Angelica isn't angelic; that big, tough-looking Sam is a timid crybaby; and that Frederick can propel a spit-wad fifteen feet with deadly accuracy.

In the course of the week, I find out things about myself as well. I realize that it is much easier to teach the principles of godliness than to practice them. I learn the joy of discovering that old, old stories can capture the wonder of a child today and that God's love knows no boundaries of age or race or culture. I learn that names on a chart grow arms and legs and personalities in a week's time and that glitter and glue wash out of almost everything.

By Friday evening, when it is time for our closing program, I am amazed that the week has gone by so quickly. I am surprised by the depth of feeling I have for "my kids" and my pride in them as they sing their songs about Noah's "arky, arky" and recite their memory verses. I watch, amused, as they lead their parents around our room, recounting the stories and projects we accomplished, proudly presenting a crooked cross made of popsicle sticks or a picture of Jesus in a frame of gilded macaroni. But I am always humbled by the few who drag their parents to my side and point to me as if I were a religious relic, announcing, "And this is my teacher. She's the one who taught me lots of neat stuff about God!"

Pamela Kennedy is a freelance writer of short stories, articles, essays, and children's books. Wife of a naval officer and mother of three children, she has made her home on both U.S. coasts and currently resides in Honolulu, Hawaii. She draws her material from her own experiences and memories, adding highlights from her imagination to enhance the story.

Expectancy

Mary E. Linton

The brown, bare feet knew well the dusty road
In summer noondays on the rural route
Where Uncle Sam's green wagon brought its load,
Creaking through waiting miles of hope and doubt.
The bare feet climbed the weather-beaten gate
And swung there waiting . . . waiting for the hour,
The eager eyes fixed where horizons wait,
Dreaming of mystic buds about to flower.
A spot of shade was good to pause a bit
And check more carefully the mailbox yield.
A breathless hush, and dancing young eyes lit
With sudden fire that leapt the distant field.
Oh, trusting, brown, bare feet that skipped their way,
Knowing that this, that this might be the day!

TIGER LILIES AND MAILBOX
Thomas H. Mitchell
New England Stock Photo

Childhood Memories

Loise Pinkerton Fritz

When twilight falls, I wander to
That home of long ago,
The treasured home of childhood days
That stood in valley low.

There is a strong affinity
Between that home and me,
For woven there were memories
And love of family.

Dear memories of helping time
When chores were to be done;
Warm memories of playing time
Beneath the bright-rayed sun.

Memories, oh the memories,
They flood this soul of mine;
Memories, golden memories
That bridge the span of time.

So is it any wonder
When twilight shadows fall,
I hear, and memory answers
The old home's whisp'ring call?

A Country Lane

Gertrude Naugler

Wake, wake with joy; the meadow dew
Is sparkling now as in the past.
Let's seek a rutted country lane
And find our old-time loves at last.

We'll go like children, breathe the scent
Of pasture land, of wooded sod
And hear forgotten morning birdsong
Or a brooklet's talk with God.

For we have changed. The rose still blooms
And opens up its fragrant heart;
But we, while wrapped in worldly cares,
Forgot to choose the better part.

The feathered jay is still as blue,
The curving buttercup as gold,
And daisies too, like gentle stars,
Bedeck the fields now as of old.

The sunlight dappling through the leaves
Shines not less warm than once it shone,
Nor are the woodland creatures now
Less dear than others we have known.

So off to the meadows strewn with dew,
To gladder skies and sweeter air.
We'll walk a rutted country lane
And find our old loves waiting there.

COUNTRY LANE
Muir Woods National Monument, California
Jeff Gnass Photography

Beyond the Garden Gate

Mary D. Benner

I lie upon a cool green bed,
A tuft of clover at my head.
A sheet of sunshine covers me,
Shadowed by leaf tracery.

The water from the garden hose
Becomes a little brook that flows.
Wilted daisies nod my way
A "thank you" for the drink today.

Three sparrows in the willow tree
Blend into a melody.
A robin views me with surprise
As I barely touch two butterflies.

I did not know I had a date
With God beyond the garden gate.
No longer do I seem to be
An isolated entity.

GRAPEVINE ARBOR
Missouri
Gay Bumgarner Photography

From My Garden Journal

by Deana Deck

THYME

"Parsley, Sage, Rosemary, and Thyme . . ."

When folk singers Simon and Garfunkel hit the radio airwaves with that classic refrain from "Scarborough Fair," I was a wretchedly uneducated gardener. The only thing I knew for certain was that zinnias would not grow in the shade. I knew this because as a college sophomore I planted a zinnia garden on the shady north side of the Victorian apartment house in which I lived; it failed miserably. Being vaguely familiar only with the herbs parsley and sage, I assumed the melancholy song referred to some romantic tête-á-tête between a lovesick boy and Rosemary, the girl of his dreams. A picnic, perhaps, or an intimate dinner party for two? Needless to say, I've learned a lot about gardening and life in general since then.

All thymes are woody perennials with tiny oval leaves. Because they are native to the Mediterranean region, they are not especially particular about their growing conditions. This is not surprising, considering that the region was formed by not-so-ancient volcanoes. The soil in the area tends to be loose and rocky, and the conditions are fairly dry. Therefore, thymes thrive in Riviera-like full sun and prefer light, alkaline soil that drains well. They need to be divided every three or four years, but divisions can be replanted easily. In general, thymes are more easily grown from divisions than from seed.

The best known variety, known as common thyme (*Thymus vulgaris*), reaches twelve to eighteen inches at full maturity. Other species are similar in size, such as lemon thyme (*Thymus citriodorus*) and silver thyme (*Thymus x. c.var. "Argentus"*). Another variety is Sicily thyme (*Thymus nitidus*), which grows in eight-inch mounds and bears tiny violet flowers in late spring. Sicily thyme in particular makes a delicious seasoning for chicken dishes. In fact, each of the thymes previously mentioned is commonly used in cooking. Thyme leaves are used primarily in poultry stuffings and meatloaf but also to flavor snapping turtle soup, clam chowder, and clam juice. Thyme is also delicious in herbed butters and when baked in herb breads. For a sweet treat, try drizzling honey that has been fla-

THYME

vored with thyme over your freshly baked bread; it is simply delectable.

Practical uses for these thymes are often found outside of the kitchen as well, especially in the healing arts. As long ago as 4000 B.C., the ancient Sumerians included thyme in their medicinal arsenal. In medieval times, thyme was prized as a cough remedy and treatment for asthma. In Shakespeare's day, thyme was even the preferred cure for nightmares.

In modern times, thyme is still used in cough drops. The herb contains an oil called thymol, known to pharmacists as an effective disinfectant and mouthwash. A pungent tea brewed from thyme, ginger, and sage is said to be an effective treatment for tension headaches and sore throats.

Gardeners choose many thymes, however, simply for their fragrance and the ornamental value of their tiny, aromatic leaves. Because of their small size, they are known as creeping thymes.

Caraway thyme (*Thymus herba-barona*), a native of Corsica, is a trailing plant that will form a dense, two-inch-high mat. When crushed, the leaves give off a delightful, caraway-scented aroma. Another popular creeper is Mother of Thyme, or *Thymus serpyllum.* It has been used in American gardens and kitchens since colonial times. These small plants are especially sought out to plant between the stones of garden paths, so that, when walked upon, their spicy fragrance perfumes the air.

In addition to their delicate appearance and fragrant aroma, thymes also have a knack for attracting bees, which adds to their popularity in outdoor gardens. I like to keep some thyme on an indoor windowsill,

Since thyme loves full sun and a soil that drains well, I pulled an old strawberry pot out of my gardening shed, cleaned it and filled it with aromatic little thyme plants that I divided from my main plant near the kitchen. How delightful!

where it's close at hand for my seasoning needs. The herb is also perfect for sweet-smelling potpourris and wreaths for your home.

In the days of knights and fair ladies, thyme was associated with the qualities of action and courage and therefore romantically linked with brave soldiers. Many a knight in shining armor rode off to defend the queen's honor bearing a scarf or scrap of fabric on which his beloved had embroidered a delicate likeness of a bee humming around a sprig of thyme. The image symbolized sincere devotion and gentleness on the part of the knight who accepted the gift.

Hmmm. If the fair lady's name was Rosemary, and the knight was leaving for a very long *time,* doesn't that mean I had it right all along? Well, maybe not; but at least I've learned more about a little herb called thyme and all its pleasant gifts.

Deana Deck tends to her flowers and vegetables at her home in Nashville, Tennessee, where her popular garden column is a regular feature in The Tennessean.

Wild Roses

Barton Rees Pogue

I've a longing for the woodland
    When wild roses are in bloom
And their fragrance fills the morning
    With a fanciful perfume,
Like as though the waking zephyrs,
    In adorning for their play,
Must have spilled a flood of perfume
    On their garments of the day.

So I hasten down a pathway,
    Round the barn and wagon shed;
For their wonderful aroma
    Has completely turned my head.
I'm as eager as a youngster
    For a future circus trip,
And the bees are all amurmur
    In the nectar they may sip.

Roses molded on this pattern
    Are old-fashioned I'll admit,
But I love their simple blossoms
    And the beauty they emit.
Not a human hand has changed them,
    Seems the Lord has piled them there
In the woodland for an altar
    And a silent place of prayer.

Handmade Heirloom

PRESSED FLOWERS from The Magic of Flowers by Jane Newdick, photography by Di Lewis,
©1989 by Salamander Books Limited, published by Salamander Books Limited, London.

Framed Pressed Flowers

Mary Skarmeas

I remember standing on my grandmother's back porch on those long ago summer days and looking with wide-eyed wonder at her beautiful garden of wildflowers. A vibrant, multicolored, living frame enclosed her small backyard and filled a little girl's dreams with pretty thoughts. I was fascinated by the infinite variety of flowers, the profusion of color and texture, the sizes and shapes of petals and leaves. From the tiniest baby's breath blossoms to the giant sunflowers, the garden's allure captivated my imagination.

Grandmother always sent me home with a small, lovingly gathered bouquet. As I watched the blooms slowly lose their color and begin to crumble, I wished that they could last forever. Perhaps these same sentiments prompted the first attempts, many years ago, at preserving flowers and immortalizing nature's bounty. Today, by carefully pressing your favorite blooms, you can actually preserve their beauty and create delicate works of art that will truly let your flowers last forever.

There has always been an appreciation for the comeliness and symmetry of flowers. Thousands of years ago, the ancient Egyptians adorned their banquet tables with floral wreaths and garlands; and early Romans scattered flower petals on the floors of their courtyards to fill the air with fragrance. These Old World customs were eventually brought to our shores; and we began to use the natural materials of the earth to please, charm, and enhance our lives. Whether it's bouquets of fragrant lilacs, perky zinnias, or romantic roses, flowers fill our lives with joy; and through the ages, we have tried to make that joy last as long as possible.

Your local librarian and bookstores have a great many books on all aspects of preserving flowers, along with dozens of suggestions for fascinating craft projects. Many people choose to temporarily preserve their flowers by simply drying them. Although a basket of dried wildflowers can be quite lovely, the blooms will eventually lose their color, dry, and crumble. But by using a simple pressing method, you can not only save the beauty of your flowers forever, but you can capture a moment in time and keep it in everyday view. Since few tools are needed and the materials are readily available, pressing flowers is an inexpensive and easily accessible project for everyone.

For hundreds of years, men, women, and children have been slipping a favorite flower between the pages of a book. Often it was to remember a loved one or a memorable occasion; other times, it was done to identify and study flora. Each new flower was carefully pressed among the pages of the family Bible or dictionary.

To properly press your favorite blooms and help them retain their vibrancy, you need to remove as much moisture from them as possible. By doing so, you can display them in a moisture-proof environment, such as a glass picture frame, and enjoy their beauty. Simply place the flowers and leaves between two pieces of absorbent blotting paper and stiff board before placing them in a flower press or between the pages of a large book. You should then let them dry from three days to several weeks, depending on the varieties of blooms you have cho-sen. Once they are thoroughly dried and pressed, carefully lift the flowers off the paper with the tip of a sharp knife.

The easiest kind of flowers to press are those with a single layer of petals, such as daisies or zinnias; but all flowers, leaves, and grasses can be pressed successfully if you follow directions carefully. While your local florist will offer many blooms and types of greenery from which to choose, your own backyard garden or a nature walk may reward you with perfect candidates for pressing.

Vivid red and blue petals seem to retain their color better than paler shades. Eventually, even the brightest, most protected flower will lose some of its color; however, it will retain enough of its vibrancy and beauty to give many decades of joy. Samples of framed and pressed flowers from the mid-nineteenth century are around today and still retain much of their original color.

After you have collected and dried your material, there are many ways in which you can create your own unique heirloom; but a framed pressed-flower picture is one of the loveliest. Using tweezers, carefully arrange your pressed flowers on the frame's background. Once you have decided on your design, dab clear, rubber-based glue under each bloom. In addition to petals, your framed picture can include a colorful spectrum of small leaves, buds, and seeds. The flowers can surround a photograph or a special poem or quote. Using your imagination and inspiration, you'll find that the possibilities are endless.

Wouldn't it be wonderful to create a lovely work of art out of pressed flowers to enhance a framed birth announcement or an anniversary party invitation? Flowers from a wedding—those that graced the church, the reception, or the bridal bouquet—can be arranged with a wedding invitation or photograph. There are so many occasions that can be personalized and preserved in an exquisite pressed-flower picture, a one-of-a-kind heirloom that will spread blossoms of cheer for years to come.

Mary Skarmeas lives in Danvers, Massachusetts, and has recently earned her bachelor's degree in English at Suffolk University. Mother of four and grandmother of two, Mary loves all crafts, especially knitting.

Country Bouquet

D. A. Hoover

He picked a primrose by the way
And saved it for his love's bouquet,
A dandelion, a clover bloom,
Petunias too and then made room
For sweetpeas from the garden wall;
An empty bottle vased them all.
His sweetheart sighed, as lovers do,
And knew his love was warm and true.

This Little Flower

Ernestine Lamont

I hold sunlight in my hand
And the moon's soft glow.
I hold day's promise, sweet and bright,
And the depth and beauty of the night.

PRIMROSE AND GAILLARDIA
Missouri in June
Gay Bumgarner Photography

Twilight

Virginia Borman Grimmer

I watch the darting fireflies
Fast lighting up the even skies
And smell the rare perfume of rose
That only summer's garden knows.

I feel the cooling nightfall breeze
Now playing tag among the trees
While scanning the bright rising moon
That quite outdoes itself in June.

I listen to the serenade,
The twilight tunes by robins played,
And wonder at this peaceful scene
When life again becomes serene.

Night Opera

Charlotte Partin

The stars hold back night's curtain.
A strobe moon shines above.
On stage, a cricket chorus
Belts out "Be My Love."

Stage left, the fireflies enter,
Ablink with evening dew.
The night owls preen and huddle,
Waiting for their cue.

Gypsy moths and mayflies
Perform "The Porch Light Fling."
In awe, the willows whisper,
Appraising everything!

A far-off dog sings back-up
To the tomcat's plaintive tune
When I attend the opera
From my back porch swing in June.

A Summer Evening

Craig E. Sathoff

A summer evening seems to be
A time to take life leisurely,
A time to walk in dusk's calm haze
And hear the cardinal's song of praise.

It calls us to the old porch swing
Where neighbors sit a-visiting.
Sometimes it means a game of ball
When sides are chosen one and all.

A summer evening after dark
Means ice-cream socials in the park
With lanterns strung from tree to tree
And town folk mingling happily.

It's time to rest at close of day
From field work and from stacks of hay
To sit in evening's gentle breeze
And savor lovely nights like these.

Sunset

Dean Robbins

A fading dandelion sun
Informs us all the day is done
As violet waves approaching nigh
Have come to flood an azure sky.
Now scarlet fire consumes the clouds;
Now silent birds, tomorrow loud.
Emerald leaves on proud display
Become a shadowed disarray
As colors acquiesce to night
And wait again for morning's light.

TWILIGHT IN THE COUNTRY
Bristol, New Hampshire
William Johnson
Johnson's Photography

Readers' Forum

Meet Our Ideals *Readers and Their Families*

ATTENTION *IDEALS* READERS: The *Ideals* editors want your "favorite memories" to share in the next issue of *Country Ideals*. Do you have a special memory of your father? Perhaps you have a cherished memory of a Fourth of July celebration or of carefree days of summertime on the farm. Send your story of about 200 typed words to: Favorite Memories, c/o Editorial Department, Ideals Publications Inc., P.O. Box 305300, Nashville, Tennessee 37230. *Manuscripts cannot be returned.*

BEVERLY CRUSCIAL sent us this summertime shot of her grandson Cameron, age twenty months, enjoying her home garden in Altoona, Pennsylvania. Cameron and his parents, Maureen McCoy and Bill Cruscial, were visiting Beverly from their home in Salem, Oregon. Beverly is an avid quilter and spends time on her hobby every day. Her other love is gardening, and young Cameron obviously shares her interest in beautiful flowers!

DELORES HUDEC of Leader, Saskatchewan, Canada, shares with us this photograph of her daughter Louise Tessier and grandson Eric, age six. The two pulled off the road near Torquay, Saskatchewan, to take a moment to enjoy a magnificent field of sunflowers. Eric's father, Larry Tessier, was the photographer; his snapshot has become one of Gramma and Grampa's favorites.

Delores works at the library in Leader, where she says *Ideals* has been delighting library patrons for years.

THANK YOU Beverly Cruscial and Delores Hudec for sharing with *Ideals*. We hope to hear from other readers who would like to share photos and stories with the *Ideals* family. Please include a self-addressed, stamped envelope if you would like the photos returned. Keep your original photographs for safekeeping and send duplicate photos along with your name, address, and telephone number to:

READERS' FORUM
IDEALS PUBLICATIONS INC.
P.O. BOX 305300
NASHVILLE, TENNESSEE 37230

ideals

Publisher, Patricia A. Pingry
Editor, Lisa C. Ragan
Copy Editor, Michelle Prater Burke
Electronic Prepress Manager, Amilyn K. Lanning
Editorial Assistant, Brian L. Bacon
Editorial Intern, Laura Griffis
Contributing Editors,
Lansing Christman, Deana Deck, Russ Flint, Pamela Kennedy, Patrick McRae, Mary Skarmeas, Nancy Skarmeas

ACKNOWLEDGMENTS
FISHERMAN from *THE FRIENDLY WAY* by Edgar A. Guest, copyright ©1931 by The Reilly & Lee Co. Used by permission of the author's estate. EARLY MORNING from *AGAINST ALL TIME* by Isla Paschal Richardson, copyright ©1957 by Bruce Humphries, Inc. Reprinted courtesy of Branden Publishing Company, Boston. Excerpt from ESPECIALLY FATHER by Gladys Taber, copyright ©1949 by Gladys Taber, copyright renewed 1975, 1976 by Gladys Taber. All rights reserved. Reprinted by permission of Brandt & Brandt Literary Agents, Inc. Our sincere thanks to the following authors whom we were unable to contact: Mary D. Benner for BEYOND THE GARDEN GATE, Myrtie Fisher Seavers for AMERICA, Charles L. H. Wagner for RHYME FOR FATHER'S DAY, Lydia Avery Coonley Ward for FLAG SONG, and Viney Wilder for PASTORAL.

Tranquility
Viney Wilder

Summer is standing still along this road
Where wild blackberries hang from dusty vines.
An ancient wagon creaking with its load
Complains to distant hills and towering pines.

The broad expanse of meadow runs to meet
The singing brook down by the pasture bars
Where patient cows have found a cool retreat
To wait for evening's first array of stars.

Time stops for just a moment to record
Tranquility against some future day,
A reservoir of peace that can be stored
And drawn upon when summer slips away.

Solace
Eleanor T. Drake

Oh, take me back and let me stand
Beside the shaded streams
Where waves and pebbles touch the land
And murmurs turn to dreams.

Reflections of the sky are cast
Deep in the quiet pond;
The scope of pleasure is so vast
I cannot look beyond.

Oh, let me find beside the rill
The solace that I love,
And let my glad heart overspill
With peace sent from above.